DESCENT IN FIVE (motions)

Tobey Hiller

Sandy Press

DESCENT IN FIVE *(motions)*

Tobey Hiller

Cover Art: *Ring the Rose* by Elizabeth Ennis

Cover design, cover preparation, interior layout
by harry k stammer

ISBN: 979-8-9924582-4-4
Printed in U.S.A.

Sandy Press
Queensland, Australia
&
California, USA

https://sandy-press.com
sandypress2021@gmail.com

Table of Contents

~One~ *Wild Flesh*   5
  The Wrong Mice   7
  Duckweed and Hemlock   12
  Kitchen Incident   17
  After the Fact   21
  Matchstick Game   26

~Two~ *Amuse Bouche*   31
  Fishbone   33
  Midnight Chips   38
  Sound Wave   41

~Three~ *Descent in Five*   43
  Descent In Five Motions   45
  Door (1)   45
  Nether (2)   46
  Show Them Who's What (3)   48
  Memory of the Future (4)   51
  Now (5)   53

~Four~ *Discursions* [Littles & Odds]   55
  Three Littles   57
  Somewhere   59
  An Essay on Time   61
  The Bath   68
  Yada Yada   72
  Hopscotch Girl   76
  That Moment   80
  Let us Entertain   82

~Five~ *How*   87
  The Small of the Year   89
  How the Moon Grew Various   95

Acknowledgments

Grateful Acknowledgment is made to the editors of the
following publications in which these works first appeared:

Fabulist Words & Art: "Memory of the Future"
Five Fingers Review: "How the Moon Grew Various"
great weather for MEDIA: "Kitchen Incident," (first publication)
and "Duckweed and Hemlock"
Ravenna Triple Series #21: "After the Fact," (with reprintings of
"The Wrong Mice" and "Kitchen Incident")
*resurgent: new writing by women (University of Illinois Press,
eds. Lou Robinson & Camille Norton)*: "The Small of the Year"
Unlikely Stories Mark V: "The Wrong Mice" (first publication)
and "Nether"
Utriculi: "An Essay on Time" and "The Bath"
Qoph: "Let Us Entertain"

"Fishbone" received *Honorable Mention* in the Humor Category
of the 2022 Bay Area Keats Soulmaking Contest

~One~ *Wild Flesh*

The Wrong Mice

He had his mother's prejudices and his father's shoulders. She liked float and specialized in drift-prone ideas, but her walk had lateral power. The first time he saw her, walking down the street right in front of him, her hips delivered a direct message right to the target. They did not swing or flick back and forth—they rolled, like the sea, and he wanted nothing more than to be a sailor on that big blue. He caught up in two steps, grinned down at her and put his supplicant hands together. He did not crowd her or speak, and she said "what?" in a tone that meant beginning.

He bought her no rings or flowers, wrote her no notes. He relied on his hands and a certain kind of winking smile. His shoulders knew what to do. The fact that she cooked for him seemed another piece of the right news. But she was not glide-right-in easy. Often, she didn't look directly at him when she talked, as though she were directing her remarks to someone standing beyond his shoulder, an alternative zone of importance just behind him. When she spoke of lottery tickets, feline memory, the aurora borealis, the way some furniture sagged too much, her glance would go galactic. Though he didn't really listen to the details, he did buy a new couch, so the hips would have a firm backing, come any high water.

So it started and continued. Nothing went wrong, though she became more quiet. A step in the right direction, as far as he was concerned. His days developed an expectation of rhythm, a slow tide of beginning, middle and end, while the nights, once darkness fell into their bedroom, flew in rumpled and wild, full of juice and feathers.

Then one day she was gone. Nobody there when he came home. No sign at all. Her things cleared out, even her kitchen stuff. He stood still in front of the couch, staring into its firm cushions. Something he didn't recognize and couldn't explain fell out of him on to the floor, and though it was invisible, he knew it was there. When he could move, he banged on the next-door neighbor's door. That leering jerk had managed to stand just a little too close and talk a little too long every time he ran into her in the hallway. Maybe she'd told him something; maybe she was even over there, just a temporary . . . But no go, despite how right it felt that she would be there, or in the closet, or on the fire escape. The guy was too relaxed to be lying, so he didn't barge into the apartment, despite how much his shoulders advised it. He went back home and sat on the couch and called her best friend, a woman with hair that stood out from her head as though electrified, shocked into aureole. But Betts hadn't heard anything. "Really?" she said. "Just like that?" He could hear her long red nails clicking on some surface as she talked. He felt the blood rush into his scalp. Maybe it was those nails, the tapping. Maybe it was that goddamn exploding hair.

That night, when he finally went to bed, he found a note under his pillow. The note said *I'm sorry, don't worry, I'm not mad.* That's all. He stared at it, kneeling on the bed. How could she . . . what? What did she have to be mad about? He tore the note in pieces, pounded the pieces into the pillow and put his face in his hands. When he went to bed, he put the phone in another room, point of pride. During the night he could have sworn he heard the phone ring, twice, but when he ran to get it, nobody, and the call record showed no one. He didn't call her. No. The next morning, he found a note in the egg carton. It said *nobody could tell you anything.* What the flying fuck did that mean? What kind of idiot leaves a note in an egg carton in the refrigerator? Those were his second and third thoughts. His first, as he slammed his hand against the side of the refrigerator, was all barbed wire bruise. He looked all over for the third note, but apparently the rule of three did not apply.

He began to hear mice scrabble in the wall at night and said out loud to himself *we have vermin.* He did not correct the pronoun. He called Betts again, and again. Then he turned up at her door, and when she opened it, he saw that her nails were short and unpolished. He couldn't help staring at her hands. He invited her over to his place, and after she had cooked dinner, they sat down on the couch. "Do you hear the mice?" he asked. "We're gonna have a stinking dead body in the walls one of these days." He didn't notice the pronoun. He stared at her. Betts looked back at him, her hair springing out like fireworks, like ragged tumbleweed, like revelation. "That's not mice," she said. "Mice thump and patter. It's willow branches scratching against the wall. Outside." Maybe it was the good news about the mice that made him kiss her. Her hair closed, a gold tickle, around his face, and whether it made a bramble or a nest or just a rest stop on a highway without road signs, his heart, still beating with the volcanic blood of yesterday, didn't know.

Duckweed and Hemlock

Selena had advised the hemlock channel, *three right turns and a curve like an eyebrow, just follow the biggest hemlock.* But in the night bayou all the channels curved and all the hemlock loomed, so Raymona followed the duckweed instead. Alligators watched the boat pass, their eyes like floating marbles on the moonlight surface of the water. Owls hooted and wooed. Bullfrogs croaked, honey bees slept gold in their tree hives. In the dark, her bruises matched shadow's colors.

The channel curved like an eyebrow and widened into pool, and there it stood, in moonlight's bright silence. Selena had called it the Queen's Tree. It stood royal above the water's stillness, wide whitened branches hung with beads, glass shards, birds of folded paper, keys, jewelry, bits of ribbon and lace. A trumpet lay in a high fork, near a doll-size rusted bedstead. She brought her canoe in close to the tree and pushed her wish, wrapped in a $20 bill, into the trunk's darkest hole, where it could not drop into water and disappear into sludge. *Get me out.* No *please*, no careful. She couldn't bear any more of that.

Going back, the duckweed had floated into different shapes, like gnats or clouds, but she found her way, no problem, drew the boat up to the dock, tied it, thanking any lucky stars that watched, and drove back. Not knowing exactly what, or how, but okay, she'd done it.

He was standing in the driveway, his hands on his hips, staring up at the roof. Flames spouted out of the chimney, climbing in curls. How had that happened? Sparks spattered off the gouts of flame, drawing firefly arcs in the air. Some settled on the roof. She smelled ash and cinder and rutilated wind. The woman who lived next door—the one who never said hello or even looked at her—ran out her front door in her bathrobe, screaming *fire!* He turned then and saw the car. And began running toward her, his mouth opening into the shape of curses. But Raymona had turned sharp left in the same instant and was two houses away.

He ran after the car, his hands pumping in balled fists, his face a blaze just as red as the flames now beginning to dribble in bright looping threads on to the roof. "Stop! Where do you think you're . . What the fu . . ? Get back here, Mona you idiot!—

that's *my* car! Stop! STOP! –you . . MONA!" She could hear

every word, including the invisible ones, clear as thunder before

lightning. She knew just what he would scream at her if the

neighbors weren't listening, if he weren't out here on the

sidewalk with other eyes on him. *Get over here with my fucking*

car, you fucking useless piece of—bitch! But those words,

plastered all over the inside walls of the house, couldn't catch up

to her out here. They choked into cinders in the smoke. She

drove just slowly enough to tempt him, her teeth clenched. She

could see him panting and flailing in the rearview mirror, along

with slow slices of the neighbors' front yards, and, farther back,

the astounding roof, now a field of roar and blaze eating the sky.

Even now, falling behind, no way to catch up, sweat popping out

on his face, he looked large, imminent, and some piece of her

mind, not a small piece, torpedoed in: *you're to blame, you did*

this, it's your fault. Again. But then, oddly, she heard her own

laugh. She looked down at her hands on the steering wheel, their

flaming fingernails. Knuckles not even white.

JeSUS! she heard Serena's voice. *Will you stop with the constant it's me, it's me? If I hadn't done this, if I'd just remembered to say that . . .Such crap! Take a look at the actual facts, will you?* She hadn't lit any fires, she knew that. But maybe they'd just flowed out of her own thought, using the painful and insistent spot behind her right ear as exit. Some moments explode into conflagration, they do. Then what? Her hands on the steering wheel felt so relaxed, and now her body felt the car, the scene, the whole story from duckweed and hemlock to now as hers—it all blazed with intention astounding as any midnight sun, proved it, lighting up the dark of then and next as clearly as a blazing house. So whether or not she believed in the Queen's Tree, and although she knew perfectly well how cheap he was about stuff like having the chimney cleaned, she wasn't going to tell Serena that. Because, okay . . . no *please,* no explanations or second guesses involved anymore, and well, here it was, the burning door she was ready to walk through.

She speeded up. She turned the corner. She leaned right and looked in the rearview mirror at her own face. Smoke in her eyes and in her nostrils, but she was smiling.

Kitchen Incident

She opened the oven door. One of the Cornish hens she was roasting flew out, brushing her arm with its seared flesh. She gasped, more of a squeak than a scream. Brown wing stubs pumping, thyme spiking out green where its head should be, it circled the kitchen, flew out the window, and off into blue, rapidly dwindling to a speck more or less like a grease spot on a favorite blue blouse.

She stared after it. 350 degrees, brown as a burned stick, flying.

She felt her mind stammer. Or was that the kitchen? Damn it all to . . .there must be something truly wrong with . . .and then she heard her mother's voice warning her, years ago, *keep that oven door closed!* whenever she had opened it to peek at whatever was cooking in there. *You'll wreck the meal!* She looked down at her arm, where a slash of red proved something, maybe the costs of betrayal. Those little hens. Their fat turned to sizzle. Wings feathered only with crisp. Was she hearing a commotion in the oven?

But now there would be only three hens in there, and four people for dinner, that was a problem she had to address immediately, *do* something said her mother's warning kitchen voice, but the reason why there were three, not four, Rock Cornish Hens seemed for god's sake like a story she couldn't tell her dinner guests. She stared at the oven door. Alec came into the kitchen, frowning. *Did I hear something? Everything all right in here?*

Oh fine, she said, *fine. Just going to baste the birds*. She pointed to the window with her oven mitt. *Could you please close the window?* He slammed the window shut, muttering *what the hell, don't you have any wings of your own?*

Arms! I have arms, not wings! she said. She looked down at herself to make sure she was telling the truth.

But she had spoken too loudly.

He glared. *What the fuck are you talking about? Of course you have arms!*

Too loud. Her ears were paper walls, not stone. There was a sizzle of cluck from the oven, she was sure of it. But how could there be cluck without beaks? She crossed her arms,

thinking feathers. At night the clanking of dreams silenced her
hungers. In the mornings, she made breakfast she made waffles
of mercy and ate the silence greedily with the spoon of a desire
whose name rhymed with tomorrow.

But it wasn't morning.

She looked down at her own hands. The oven mitts
warned her. She yanked open the oven door. To hell with her
mother. And one after another, they flew out, little wing stubs
flapping, the sprongs of green thyme like antennae above their
brown shoulders, reaching for distance, reaching for blue. Alec
staggered back. *Open the window, open the window!* she
shouted, and to his credit, he did. And then turned in mesmerized
half-circles, first staring at her, then out the window.

She herself walked out through the front door, untying
her apron, spreading her fingers into air like petals, sailing
smooth through the staring silence, the round o's of all their
mouths, the last sizzle of her own doubts. A distant yammer of
her mother's voice faded fast, as the garbled sounds of wonder or
sorrow, she didn't know which, came loud from behind her,
where Alec stood in the kitchen doorway. When she got out

under the trees, she lifted her arms, the feather weight of them. She reached easily up toward that other home, the blue. She paid no attention to the noisy silence behind her. She would join her own flock.

After the Fact

When she opened the door, she thought she saw a bear standing

there. But then her last night's dream, which had involved a

violent but transforming encounter—blood, love, rumble of

furred running—yes, with a bear! cleared. Just a tall guy, after

all, with long, tangled hair, rumpled clothes, long fingers—

squint and well yeah, they did have a sort of clawed curve and

gleam, you had to admit, but really. . . Anyway, he was holding

a package against his chest. Involuntarily, still shivered with the

dream's after-effect facts, she took a step back. He held out the

package. His arm, brown curve of something gentle, pierced her

hesitance. Which was centered somewhere in her chest,

uncomfortably close to her heart.

Automatically, she took it. That was probably her first

mistake, she thought later, but her dream did not agree.

"Excuse me." He smiled, another quick gleam of

sharpened white. Her shoulders tightened. "May I use your

bathroom?" She blinked; his nose had a snout-y look, didn't it?

His voice was perfectly modulated, no growl or burr, but that didn't help.

"What?" But he smoothed right by her, somehow making his large body—was he wearing some kind of furry jacket?—slip by without touching her. Every hair on her body awoke. He walked down the hall, pigeon-toeing along in a strange slouchy gait, and disappeared into her bedroom as though he knew exactly where to go. Her bedroom door of dream. Shortly, she heard the toilet flush.

That was it, she told herself. She walked partway down the hall. "Sir? Um, mister . . . would you please . . .this isn't . . ."

He emerged from the bedroom door and stood, towering, about five feet away. He had large pointed ears, or was that some sort of cap? Good god.

"Why don't you open the package?"

"Please leave."

He didn't move. "Open the package. It's for you. You."

"I—listen, thanks for delivering this, but now you've done your job, and—" she gestured toward the door.

He loomed closer, peering at her with large, liquid eyes. She backed up against the wall and began, though she tried to hide it, to tremble.

"I have to make sure the delivery is to the right person. Open the package before I go." In fact, his voice was quite deep, and now graveled, somewhere south of baritone. But not unpleasant. Sort of like macadamia nuts, unsalted.

She looked down at the small package in her hand, wrapped in reddish-brown paper. She saw her name written on it in a loopy hand. No address. She swallowed, her throat dry as when you know you're about to say something you never meant to say. Maybe if she humored him. But what if the package contained something dangerous, like anthrax, snoozing but soon-to-awake killer wasps, or—but what was she *thinking*?—a command she couldn't resist? She tried to read the future in the odd hieroglyphic of her written name, which didn't help.

Here you are talking to a loon in your own hallway, the voice outside of her dream said.

"Don't worry." His large eyes blinked, as though he had read her mind, and now his voice was as green as small wind in the trees. "It won't hurt you. Really. Just a package for you to open."

She stared at him. How did you ever know, anyway? At that moment, he looked as warmly brown and steady as any Oak.

She opened it. That was her second mistake. If that's what you want to call it. Mistakes are always a question after the fact.

Inside the package lay a scarf, some brown, plush material. She lifted it out. He made a soft grunting sound—was that a laugh?—and cocked his head to one side. "Try it on, why don't you?" He had not moved forward, but now his hands were pressed against his chest, large fingers shadowed with hair, almost supplicant. She felt stuck in place, as though her feet had become very heavy. She looked down at them. They seemed oddly large. A breeze grazed her cheek. The air in the hallway seemed too narrow, and she glanced upward, wondering where the sky had gone. She wrapped the scarf around her neck. That was her third mistake, but by that time she was arranging the word "mistake" into another language made of a substance like earth and the smell of water, and so it simply meant *now*.

She felt the scarf attach itself to her skin, her limbs, her life, a soft pelt with all her forest and blood memories attached. She felt the lengthening, the sharpening.

"Bingo!' he said in a brown, growly voice, and now she saw his claws, his teeth, the muscle of all his intentions. "I knew you'd look great in fur!"

Matchstick Game

The doom fairy, resembling a small contraption made of soot, with many mechanical limbs and a blipping screen up top, lays them down in a row, bottoms all precisely aligned. Seven wooden matchsticks. The tips flame red. Althea's hair is the very same color, a vermilion dragon-coxcomb flare; the curly ends sizzle. Though Althea enjoys this game, she has no expectation that this opponent will play by the rules, so she doesn't wait for the doom fairy to lay the next line. She picks up six of the seven matches and drops them in the glass of water at her elbow. The doom juggernaut laughs with an almost-human mouth—a flash of teeth on the empty screen that is its head—and knocks over the glass. Water drips on to Althea's bare foot. A wet matchstick gets caught between her big toe and the next one. She glances down, scrunches her foot and flicks it away.

But when she looks up from her wet foot, though it has only been a splashed moment, two matchsticks have appeared on the table, one above the other. It has all happened much faster than her mother told her it would. Not the only thing her mother had said that didn't work out, but Althea tends to blame that on her father, who laid a lot of land mines along the path—she's no stranger to sudden tangents in the narrative. Before the doom fairy can take her turn, Althea sweeps the two remaining matches apart on the table, one far to her left, one far to the right. She leans this way, that. The doom fairy opens the clanking cave of its mouth, and out of it blows a great wind. But quicker than you can say lickety-split, Althea scoops up the two matchsticks and puts them in her mouth, holding them cowpoke-wise between her teeth, one pointing north, one south, and, helped by the cloud of wind that now encircles her, begins to dance.

Though the ground tilts beneath her feet, and her dance is off-kilter and adulterated with memory's unforgiving knobs of gravity, sending her here and there and who knows where, she is used to this motion. She rolls the matchsticks back and forth across her lips, and, more or less by accident—but who knows what's accidental when it comes to the body's decisions, made like unexpected rock slides or puffs of wind already blowing off your hat?—she swallows one. The other drops away and flies off into the wind's throat.

Immediately, Althea finds herself balanced and whirling steadily to the left—that is, in the direction of her own heart, her arms out wide, her axis as firm as any wheeling galaxy. Inside her, the renegade matchstick abjures fire and remembers wood.

Out of Althea's left palm and fingers there grows a branch, and then from her head a green and leafy crown unfolds, and slowly but surely, she becomes brown and green and rooted, turning in the exact center of the great wind's eye. Of course the doom fairy—no surprise here—flies in with its claptrap wings and hides in the growing maze of her branches. But, since all the matches but one have disappeared or been used up, Althea may have fooled the doom fairy into taking a breather, won the matchstick game and saved the world, for now. Whether or not this is true, whether this state of things will last into next, is something you and I will never know.

Inside Althea, the renegade matchstick often dreams of an earlier volcanic life in which the red beauties of conflagration and churn burn bright, but, upon waking to a daily green, remembers again how air is now its motive, not its food. The wood of it grows roots.

~Two~ *Amuse Bouche*

Fishbone

Once upon a time my mother got a fishbone stuck in her throat. She was chewing and talking at the same time—not an uncommon occurrence—and down it went. She stood up and ran into the kitchen, saying something gargly. My father followed her. "Easy, easy," he said, patting the air with his hands. "Now don't swallow. Whatever you do, don't swallow."

But she swallowed. "Get in the car," my father said. "We're going to the hospital."

"No, we're not," she said.

"It's a fishbone," said my father.

"*I* swallowed it, Arthur!"

"I know! That's why we're going to the hospital!"

"Bread! Bread!" said my mother and began to tear up large quantities of bread and stuff it into her mouth.

"There," she said, chewing, still bent over, her face pointing toward the kitchen floor as though the bone might still reverse its chosen and lethal course down her throat and pop out on to the linoleum, "there. I'm sure it's gone now."

They went on arguing for a while about whether to go to the hospital, but I stopped listening. I could tell from the tone of my father's voice that he had no intention of going anyway at this point and had probably never had any real intention of going.

The whole idea of the hospital had just erupted into the hullabaloo as a sort of penalty because she had swallowed, foolishly, when he told her not to. She herself would probably have insisted on going to the hospital if my father hadn't mentioned it. They were like that. They each wanted to advise, but neither wanted to consent. Sometimes it steered clear of rancor, sometimes not; but it was a form of daily labor, like herding piebald ponies and striped zebras with a tendency to commingle, causing traffic jams and shadowy tangles, to opposite sides of the corral. They each seemed to think they had lots of extra knowledge, and they needed to off-load it on to someone or other. What's the use of knowledge, anyway, if you can't get someone else, by the application of a little informational heft, to do something they otherwise would never have considered doing in a million years?

In any case, three weeks later, when my mother did go to the doctor, complaining of a scratchy throat, and told him about the fishbone, he looked at her severely. I know. She had dragged me along with her for "moral support."

"What kind of a fishbone, Mrs. Trimble?"

"Uh, salmon."

"The very worst kind. Tiny, flexible bones, hard to find. They can lodge anywhere: esophagus, lingual ridge, under a tooth, anywhere. And they're loaded with bacteria. Often cause a septicemic reaction."

"Oh dear."

"Did you go to the emergency room?"

"No."

He frowned. "Well. Let's take a look." He grabbed her tongue with a gauze pad and looked down her throat with a little mirror. My mother, meanwhile, concentrated on not gagging.

By the end of the visit, she had been convinced that it had been a lucky chance she was still among the living. On the way home, she made me promise to "let her handle this." Which meant keep quiet. I knew her actual motive in dragging me was to make me a witness, though to what, given her apparent brush with death, a situation predicted by my father, it was now unclear.

At home she announced, triumphantly, "the fishbone's out. The doctor said it might have killed me!"

My father said, "didn't I tell you we needed to go to the hospital? Didn't I?"

"It was a case," she said, her enunciation very distinct, "of crossed wires. You said this, I said that. But as I told Isabel—" she pointed to me—"doctors are so used to crisis that it's possible, now that I think of it, that he was exaggerating just a little bit. And anyway," spreading her arms wide, "I didn't die, did I?"

"No," said my father, raising up his newspaper, "which, all in all, is a good thing. Otherwise I'd have to feel both vindicated and tragically deprived. This way I simply feel vindicated and, as usual, ignored."

"In any case," she said, "not tragically ignored." She waited. She was fishing.

He shook the paper, but there was a little twitch at the corner of his mouth.

"That's true. Lucky for us both that whatever being right and being ignored deprived me of, it wasn't my wife."

My mother, showing unusual restraint, said nothing.

And that was the last of that fishbone.

Midnight Chips

Wee hours: plush dark. Stars hover up there, rooftop garden. Warm bed. Mild snores next to you. But you're definitely not sleepy. So you rouse the dreaming man beside you and whisper "potato chips!" in his left ear. He springs into immediate action, for there are just two things he's always ready for—morning, noon or night—and one is making and eating delicious food together. No doubt you can guess the other.

In the kitchen, both of you, half naked and salivating, get out the supplies. He slices potatoes almost paper thin with the wooden Japanese slicer perfect for this operation. Meanwhile, a half inch of oil is heating in a deep frying pan. He slips the slices into the oil and they begin to darken to a golden color, the thin brown edges crisping and curling. The sound is of bubbles and brim: all you have to do is keep the spat under control. You spread out paper towels, double-thick, and as each batch comes out of the oil, you spread them on the towels to dry and harden. They glow golden as large succulent coins. You turn them. You salt them lightly. They curl a bit, lie there temptingly, miniature midnight suns waiting to prove to you both that the world, day or night, is sweet salt and oily, with a perfect crust of crunch and a homemade perfection only you, each of you together, can achieve, all in an improvised moment of shared desire.

You stand at the counter and eat and laugh and feel, together, that these midnight chips are the best meal you've ever had. While above you, I say, the stars wheel, the unseen clouds pass by, the moon, as usual, does not blink, and in all the nearby houses (at this succulent moment you don't bother to imagine this, but here we can hope) some little chip of this kind of happiness may soon arrive, morning, noon or night.

RECIPE: Midnight Chips

Ingredients:

2 russet potatoes, washed, dried and sliced very thin with a
Benreiner (a Japanese wooden slicer)

    or a mandoline

light oil good for deep frying

salt to taste

Heat a quarter to half an inch of oil in a deep frying pan till hot
enough to deep fry but not hot enough to jump out of the pan and
attack you. Batch by batch, keeping the slices from lying on top
of each other, fry them till golden brown. Remove the slices to
paper towels placed on plates or board to dry and drain off
excess oil. Turn them to dry and drain both sides. Lightly salt to
taste. When the chips are cooled and crisp, put them on a plate,
sit down together, or stand at the counter, and feed each other
delicious midnight potato chips.

Sound Waves

He is a man in frequent disagreement with his equipment—
electronic, digital, metallic, whatever. Stuff thwarts him. Things
don't go smoothly, he doesn't read directions, someone has
stolen or misplaced his tools, some unexpected snafu arises. He
puts in the wrong date. His password doesn't work. He deletes
the form by mistake. The pipe breaks, the toilet leaks. Though he
remains confident in his technical expertise, and indeed has
some, somehow he often meets with mysterious barriers to the
straightforward, relaxed and easy accomplishment of his
projects.

These experiences are accompanied by an audible running
monologue of questions, ruminations and exclamations that seem
to invite outside help or comment. There is a tinge of
desperation. But beware suggestion or remark. Though he's
talking out loud, and the surrounding atmosphere fills to a
ballooned pressure of loud voice, this cloud of puzzled irritation,
anxiety, imprecation, and curse is a dangerous environment to
enter. He's waiting to explode. Any suggestion or comment is

fire to a fuse. So even though he's talking and seems to be telling the story of his experience to some audience, perhaps you, don't say anything. Silence is best. Or disappearance entire.

Though there may be no way to solve the question of whether a tree falling in the forest makes a sound when no creature with ears is present, it is a confirmed fact that when no one's nearby he does not talk out loud. This leaves two questions. What makes a sound wave sound? Only ears, it seems. And is his flustered soliloquy when someone is present simply a provocation to any listener, a means of releasing the bubble of anger and sending it into some other body? Could this be another kind of wave, too, colored red or itchy or webbed, like a spider's construction? You tell me. Maybe I'll hear you.

~Three~ *Descent in Five*

Descent in Five Motions

Door (1)

She sat up. Had there been a noise? The bedroom was dark, except for the pencil-thin line of light around the blind, cast by the streetlight. The cat's weight against her foot didn't shift. Had it been a door opening? She listened. Nothing.

Okay.

Carefully, not to disturb the cat, she folded back the covers and rose, feeling a bit dizzy. The floor felt furry, as though still made of dream molecules. She turned right at the bottom of the bed and followed a familiar pathway across the rug toward the unlit bathroom. Felt for the door, entered. Felt for the toilet seat. Cool air against her waving hand. Stepped forward. Stepped forward again. Again. She stopped. Steps at her feet, just visible now in the darkness, leading downward.

A cool wind from below.

Without hesitation, knowing she didn't know where she was, she started down. Thinking *is this a beginning, or an end?* And then she felt, at her feet, the cat. He was coming, too.

Nether (2)

It was a dark and stormy noon. Lightning struck the front door. It flamed and crumbled to ash. In he walked. He towered, he stuck out his lower lip, he reached out a surprisingly small hand with gilt fingertips. His blond pompadour obscured his eyes.

-You're going to love me. I know everything about you. Which is your deepest crevice?-

Breathing seemed the best option, despite the stench. It had been years since she'd eaten a pomegranate, but she remembered the taste, red as blood.

-Come over here.- She patted the couch and smiled, demure curve. Behind the couch—it had been there a long time, and sometimes a wintery wind blew up from there—was the stairway down. She'd kept her kids from going back there, but now . . .

He sat down, grinning, and reached for her right breast with his gilded hand. The cat ran out of the room.

-Wait. Follow me! I know a better place.-

And she rounded the couch, just shy of his plucking hand, and ran down the dark stairway. *No stumbles*, she ordered her feet, *no stumbles. Ruthless, quick.* (Whose words were that?) He panted behind her, surprisingly agile despite his paunch, his fat ass. Some mutter, then the roar: *do you know who I AM?* Gravel, a dark wind against her face. She would shut the door as he rushed past; she saw it ahead now. And then. She'd call the guard, the one with three heads (one head understood forest maneuver, one counted circles of hell, and the third had mapped the maze at the center of the earth). She remembered his name still: Caliban. Though half-covered in bark and tattooed by scorn and history's ugliness, this guardian was faithful to light.

She ran, at each step a seed sprouting.

Show Them Who's What (3)

He steps (should he be running, sweeping, waving?) through a door. Feeling not quite like himself. More like someone too far from lunch, more like the paste he'd always eaten in 3rd grade. He could remember that kid he'd tried to throw out the window, but he had no idea if he'd liked eating paste too. Probably not. He was a loser.

Anyway, soon as he gets through the door, a red carpet appears, as promised. But it branches, or whatever you call it when the map turns into a math equation. Crap. Too many exits and entrances. Too many signs with no neon and too many words. Boring. Also a little scary. Just go ahead and grab that . .

He pictures a couple of her melons, plump under his . . .

Okay. There. That guy, the rumpled but smart one, waving him over there. So he goes. Over there. There's the microphone. The roaring and applause convince him. Though for crapssake, it's all more than you could expect anyone who knows how to run something be in charge I can tell you that believe me would pay attention to. He smiles at a guy in the back row. They love me. But the path squirms like a snake under his feet. Holy shit. Maybe that white thing is a golf ball?

He exits to the right. Couldn't have been a golf ball. Oh no! Could it have been one of those miniature drone-bomb things they keep telling him about? He scowls. Let's get things back on track, ok?—gilt-bargain signposts shining and also a fuckin' hamburger for crapssake.

Good time, that's it, to pick up the phone. Wait— tropical or tundra? World class hotel on an iceberg, penguin dinners. Great idea. Look at them out there, all waving banners and hats. You're beautiful people! The rumpled guy nodded and gleamed (somewhere back there; someone else is yammering at him now). So true. When you know what you're doing, you do it. Don't wait. Which means fire that little rat-faced guy. Fire his ass. And the one always telling him "no no you can't do that" with his nothing but frowns. Lock him out or in or up, that'll do it. Another loser.

He raises his right arm. The air told him to wave. Obviously, it approves.

The red carpet is looking navy blue. Or is it getting dark? Downward into the shadow is not his preferred direction, but the gravel makes it a bit slippery. Hard to stop.

Far off to the left is a low burr, maybe a growl. Something white, maybe a bird or model airplane, flies at him, lands at his feet. Ah crap. He sees what it is. He frowns. Then grins. No problem! He tears up the newspaper, balls it up, squeezes hard, looks at the bits and pieces of words in his hand. Sort of like burned French fries with mayo. He eats the clump. When it comes out the other end, it'll be digested. Then he'll post it.

Far off to the left, grumble seethes. He glances over. A shadow, of a massive female figure with one arm thrust into the air. A feeble light flickers in her hand. He ignores her—after all, she's needed serious reconstruction for a long time, and she can't walk. Okay. Let's move along here. He thinks of the noble sound the helicopter makes when he lifts off, eating a burger. The furry static buzzing on the horizon doesn't matter, probably just a fake sound effect anyway. His motto has always been: what you don't know should move to Sweden.

Memory of the Future (4)

He sat in a gilt chair. His chariot had stalled in a rancid fog, which reduced visibility to 20 feet.

-Tule fog!- His voice had teeth. -It will clear in a minute! If it doesn't, we'll sue!-

But particles of soot rained from a black sky, and the coal tar in our nostrils, along with the stench, made it hard to breathe.

-Do you like my helmet?- His smile showed a flash of dagger tooth.

-*Yes! Yes! Yes!*- The crowd shouted in unison. Four or five people collapsed from the effort.

-Do you like my scepter? Beautiful, huh?- He lifted his golf club.

More affirmative shouting. The crowd stood on the prone bodies of the people who had collapsed, gasping like beached fish, beneath the trample.

-Do you like my cabinet?- He opened a box on the seat next to him. Inside were three small figures about the size of

Punch and Judy marionettes, two men and a woman. One, a gray-haired man in rumpled clothes and glasses, looked up and grinned. He raised a blunt-nosed handgun and pulled the trigger. *Bang!* Out shot a white flag with the words *Heil It*! into the air.

The crowd roared. Right hands soared upward into a forest of fingers.

The second man, in a dark suit, didn't smile or move. He was sitting on a large pile of money. He stared at a phone in his left hand, frowning. In his right hand he held a crumpled newspaper. Or was that a ball of caramel corn?

These two disappeared in a ball of smoke. Magic?

The third little puppet, the woman, was blonde in the same way platinum and yellow diamonds are blond. In fact, maybe her hair was made of Rumplestilskin's pale promise. (Where the needle was no one knew.) She was dressed in a white dress trimmed with crystals, and her belt was rust. She smiled and stepped out of the cabinet in 4-inch heels on to his lap, careful to miss the places that might cause pain or some kind of enlightenment. She nestled in, purring like a cat.

Everyone cheered. She waved and held up a contract in Chinese. Or maybe Cyrillic.

In the distance, the moan of ice, the roar of fires, the long howl of a wolf. The trees said words they had reserved for warning. The sky ached a certain gray. Minerva, in the form of an owl, entered stage left. She flew low and in utter silence over him, over the crowd and out of the picture.

Now (5)

I sit up in bed.

Middle of a dark night stretched into worlds.

Broom of virus sweeping. Falling towers.

Green seeping into air's tornado.

How many seeds have we eaten?

Is there a door?

~Four~ *DISCURSIONS* [Littles & Odds]

Three Littles

~Inauguration~

When you are a child, you sometimes eat interesting and strange food at other people's houses. Then your mouth tells you there's some other life that tastes and smells and feels completely different.

Just around the corner, just down the
block.

~Keys, Cat, Cupboard~

She put the keys in the empty honey jar. Something belonged in there, and it wasn't bees. It wasn't as much humph as it was her shoulders laughing. It was still funny, wasn't it? She didn't put the cat in the cupboard. She wasn't that far gone. More chuckle shoulders. *Age*—she thought this—I know, because who knows I may turn into her—*is like static in the tissues. Bits of glass and grumble* (this is already true) *where all slid smooth before. Distant thunder in the moment's cup.*

~Card Trick~

You thought you knew. Me, too. Robin Hood and Annie Oakley,

Sitting Bull, they had a book of knowledge made of green and

arrows. Remember how the card trick's fun because you *don't*

know? Though what you don't know can really hurt you, don't

forget. It's a puzzle. Some people are good at them, but still it's

the same: the future doesn't care what you think you know.

Knowing's cracked up to be the spine of action, but I'd say that

spine's desire. Even in the green no brown nut knows anything

but swell.

                                    What I knew was tree limbs,

gallop, wind. Those I knew.

Somewhere

Story jumped out of bed. Trying to remember its dream, it rushed around like a woman in mid-life trying to get her children off to school, prepare dinner early, find a fresh shirt in the dryer and shovel herself out the door to work. On the way, employing her native sleight of hand, story changed transportation: car to space module. She landed on Mars (yes, now *she*, Story'd never been attached to any particular spot or splice on the gender scale, though there were only seven ways to find the forest of Arden and one of them was known only to the oldest living orangutan, who spoke a number of languages besides her native orange, and as for respiration beyond Earth's atmosphere, no space suit required—Story was used to breathing fire, to airless caves, to mermaid's ocean lung and the sun's relentless pixels painting her heart blue, so forget worry about her survival.)

She looked around for a thread. A ball of yarn, a stray algorithm, floating spider filament, whatever. She knew she'd left a whole pile fermenting somewhere. Maybe back there in that cave, where Min. (—atour ? –nie Mouse?) Monster breathed out fire and desperation? A wing and a prayer, was that the one?

Maybe. A falling tower? An oud whose every note was pearls

and honey? A gilt toilet whose flush was the event horizon of a

black hole's gulp? flushing down a miniature world the

inhabitants had thought too large to enter that abyss? No, no, a

scissors. A spindle. Maybe a sieve. Better yet, a bucket and

hatchet. There'd be gold in Mars' invisible rivers. And thieves

shaped like sand dunes, of course. Always thieves. Always sweat

and silk and mud. Blood and thunder. And dishes to do.

An Essay On Time

It was a dark and stormy afternoon. The bedroom held it.

Outside, the slough was goosebelly silver and the meadow

reflected greenish light; inside the air hung blurred, fogged with

words. The color of this had no feathers.

It was a dark and stormy moment. Would it pass? Moments are

eager to go, though some return. The drumbeat of this one

rippled into the room's time, which, like the sea, had tides.

The question is going to be where to find the beginning. The

middle's easy—we're always in it. Until the end, of course—

when the middle coagulates into a story already told, in versions.

It's the beginning that disappears over an event horizon that

might be, when you take a good look, dark and stormy. Or, blink

again, on the other hand dazzling, in fact auroral. Dawn's a daily

story, married, as eye to eyelid, to dusk. There are different

views, it's clear, and they're not limited to these two moments of growing or fading light—you can't escape variety in the landscape. It's time that unrolls the conundrums.

In this dark and stormy moment, she thought mainly of escape, or a quiet that resembled torpor, the scent, for instance, of tropical ginger. His voice like a helmet she wished to remove. He thought mainly of his fury, his chest and throat, what she was costing him. He regarded himself as a man who kept his eye on the ball, not as a man beside himself. She thought of herself sometimes, and possibly in this moment, as a bird or cat, two creatures, you will note, whose cohabitation works only when there's plenty of room. No doubt they both had their reasons, or at least some map for the pathways they'd followed into this moment; still, reason is rarely a feature of conflict. She felt his pathway narrow and rocky, with walls that cut off a wider view. He was not interested in any goddamn pathway metaphor.

It may be pertinent here to mention the trembling gap between stories and lies. And the fact that time is factless and unwinged. Stories ride it; lies like it too. That no philosophy comforts, unlike trees. Are these dark and stormy thoughts? Not the tree part. I am doing the best I can, with the words time has given me. They gather in tribes, like moments. As for stories, some lope along, or tick and then explode. Some know what a galliarde is, or a joke, and I prefer these, to tell the truth. They are all around us, revealed on time's uncalendared skin. Lies, too, hatch constantly, though you might be able to tell them by the fact that their eggs stink. Of course, that's true of some facts, too.

So now, you see, as always happens in the grip of time, we are confused.

In this dark and stormy moment, she thought mainly of another life, with a scent like tropical ginger. What he thought had no scent and was all airborne, reverberating in its own life. They both thought mainly of themselves as misunderstood. The easy cohabitation of the past and the future clashed in this moment's velocity, despite earlier clues to the contrary. To both of them, this made the room seem smaller than the emotional space required. She watched some shadow disappear around a corner

that did not exist. The door he was about to slam stepped

forward. This was no surprise to either of them. No doubt they

both had their reasons, or at least some map for the pathways

they'd followed into this moment; still, reason is so rarely a

feature of connection, which, like time, is a conundrum, and has

tides. She felt his current reasons narrow and rocky, with walls

that cut off a wider view. He was not interested in her reasons at

all.

But I am repeating myself, more or less.

Looking at a room blurred with time, you may glimpse the

specks and glitters of multiple moments—these include many

stories, any lies, the prickly touch of some dark unknown, and

the breast of truth, feathered yes and breathing, such a fragile

bird, so soon flown. Time, then, as a skin, a nest, a figment.

Perhaps it seems a whirlwind, or a musical chord, or simply a

cave where you need a flashlight to see the markings.

Even in the matter of love, which also has its tides, its

imperatives, its desertions of the expected physics, you need a

flashlight to see the markings. So often illegible, despite all the

sonnets. She had meant to tell him that, but did not find the

words, just as he had meant to tell her where to find the ball,

which had rolled under some table somewhere in the course of

dinner and lost its way.

Time's hand appears everywhere. Though of course time has no

hand. Or skin, etc. It is not even an equation at the speed of light.

Always the inescapable language of our own bodies. Time has

no body, though our bodies tick with time's blood pulse. It does

not run, or stop or wait, or hold, or die or breathe or wonder. Or

love. But we are lost in it as completely as if it were a body

much larger than ours, say a sea. A sea offering what seems an

endless immersion that ends, finally, on the rocks or sand.

When he turned toward the door, the hand of an invisible heft,

perhaps feathered but stubborn, brushed him back. Or perhaps it

was the disappeared ball, landing hard between the blades of

his mind's shoulders. So he made instead a bargain with his
mouth, to let no words pass, for how many hours he did not
count or imagine. He would consider the word "pathway,"
which had come to him as an emanation of dusk's air. She,
meanwhile, watched the goosebelly silver of the slough turn
blue, and at the bluest moment, all pathways seemed ready to
lead to the curiosities and certitudes of Rome, beckoning.
Though no destination was needed, and no map, only this blue.
She felt him standing still, as the door, through which evening
blew in, turned into time, which has no direction.

You will note that words run away like love or time, even though
you can read them over and think they've helped you snag a
stitch of stillness. What enters you is feathered. Another of
time's conundrums. Being made of time, I cannot help trying to
say it. Just like you, I can only assume. While I count the fingers
on the past's left hand, the right hand holds up the goodbye of
things.

A color of invisible feathers in which we fly.

time equals but is nothing the same as
rock

river   orbit

constellated space

a thrown baseball   the

doeppler effect

and

whale fall

whose bodies falling full fathom five

to a deep we cannot survive

harbor whole

civilizations   teeming cities   forests

of small creatures, blooms and

biologies

we cannot imagine

time is nothing that comes after *is*
it is something that comes after *be*..

The Bath

Many nights she took a bath, late. By that time things were over. She closed the door to the bathroom, drew the bath, and lay back in the warm waters, subsiding into another medium than the day's piled-up hours. As though—she did not *think* this, just knew it in the water's lip and smooth—to be engulfed in a cloud of her own unknowing. Unknowing, that is, about anywhere but right here, unknowing about noon or morning insistence, other rooms and their corners, lists, hullabaloo minor or major.

Warm float, that's all she wanted. She dreamed the door to the bathroom a moat, the cloud of thoughtlessness a bulwark of handy air. Handfuls of calm. First the rushing sound of the tub filling. Then quiet, a few drips from the faucet, which in these moments had a plucked but soft sound of mermaid melody, a feel of melt on a watery edge. Occasional lapping sounds when she moved. Tides. Her mind would empty as she lay in the water, eyes closed. She always put a washcloth soaked in the hot bath water over her exposed chest to keep it warm. Her mother, who had not taught her much that was useful, had taught her this trick, and when she laid on the washcloth, her mother invariably came to mind. Also when she saw certain blues. Her mother had loved a particular blue whose name she could no longer remember—it may have begun with an a or a p—or maybe some other runaway letter—but was neither azure nor periwinkle and had now disappeared into a nameless ocean of muted blues—like so much about her mother, who had been so, yes, blue. For years she herself had never worn blue. Silly. The water in the tub, a faint greenish color, was far from the triumph of lapis seas, of course. Different waters everywhere, a reminder. When the washcloth cooled, she warmed it again in the water and laid it down, a comfort to her heart, once more. Her hands floated. The cloth weighed down her breasts with warmth. She lay unmoving for long minutes, in the embrace of what seemed a heavier and kinder air. A kind of sensate music. Sometimes she dozed. It was always hard to make the decision to get out, but. But next was always there, so eventually she'd wash herself and climb out, towel off, apply cream, brush her teeth, all that stuff. It was the bath that counted. The bath that offered a little door, like a creek carrying your thoughts around a bend, to something she didn't even have to name.

Maybe three nights out of seven she managed this. Not every night worked—hard, often, to fit it in, what with life's imperatives outside the bathroom. She did not think of the bath and its soothing waters, though, as an escape, more as a right, a bonded pleasure, a sinking into water's cerulean music, a respite too often shortchanged by schedules and stridencies—of hurry and plan, the demands, both explicit and implicate, others made on her, anticipation's push or strive, the news, her own hopes unfurled like flags, the hours that tolled and beeped, devices that reminded. It all spoke and trilled and buzzed and clicked. Or shouted. Far too much noise and muscle in every air. Too hard to hear the other music.

The frequency changed. It became four nights out of seven, and then, over time, five. The baths became longer; she had begun to lock the door, though—for reasons having to do with the time of night—knocking was rare.

It was how to come and go, daily, that snagged every moment. How to stay or say. Or not. But in the waters of the bath what wandered in and out of mind's air, or flew away to roost somewhere, in its own froth, splash or ripple, grew easy. She craved this more and more, like food or sleep or sky's free clouds. No sharp tangles occurred in the bath. An evening ocean, and she lay in a little ship on waters that did not insist on travel. Yet.

It was the day she filled the tub so full it began to splash over on to the floor she had just that morning mopped that she realized the ship had set full sail.

At last, she thought. A simple motion, neap tide and all in balance. She rose out of the tub, dried herself, applied the usual cream, dressed, and walked out of the bathroom and straight out the front door, leaving the aqua mermaid sheen of her wet footprints on the bathroom floor, where they dried before anyone saw them.

Yada Yada

He was not a man who liked to listen to other people's stories. When they started in, he did one of two things. #1: Leave the room to visit the bathroom. #2: Chuckle (to bulwark his roadblock with warmth) and interrupt at a plausible point to tell his own story. He was almost always interested in his own stories.

Some of his stories contained cameras. His favorite, which he decided to tell tonight, was about the time he dropped his Fuji off an Egyptian camel into the sand and only later realized that the camera he'd dug out of the sand and cleaned with some difficulty was not his own and had a different set of pictures in it than he'd taken, though it was exactly the same make and series as his own. Very odd, he commented (as always, there was a rhythm, a gathering theme and variation, well-practiced, to these stories), but no doubt the explanation did not include extra-terrestrials. (He chuckled. A little joke always added to the flow.) The photos in this found camera featured a woman wrapped in a lovely shawl; in some pictures, only her eyes and dark hair could be seen. They had a seductive quality, these photos, though, he said, knowing the importance of drama and mystery, she did not look happy.

"So what was the story of these found artifacts?" he asked whoever was listening, most of them by now doubtless in the palm of his hand. "What happened?" This was rhetorical: he himself intended to answer this question. With color and verve, which is what would distinguish his answer from any of theirs. His favorite version involved an American woman on vacation kidnapped by two men, a story he'd once heard from a woman he'd known long ago who had actually been abducted from an Egyptian market. It was a dark but ultimately satisfying tale containing blindfolds and terror, bravery and wiles on her part, minimized blood and bruises, and an ending with a release on a dark road, and a long, footsore trip back to a more acceptable reality. Just what any listener wanted. He did not go too deeply into any explanation of why the woman in the found camera appeared in those photos wrapped in a shawl, striking typically Arabian Nights poses.

"What do you mean 'what happened?' To the camera or the woman?" one of his female listeners said this evening, frowning, disregarding the rhetoricality.

"Ah, but here's where the story takes a turn!" he said, getting ready to tell his tale.

"I found a role of film on a Hawaiian beach once," she replied, apparently applying some thieving techniques of her own to the conversation, "and when I got home and developed the film there were all these pictures of jellyfish and a few of some young Hawaiian kid with wet hair and a ragged swimsuit, frowning at the camera—" and then some other woman chimed in (it was always women) "—this reminds me of all those dispossessed old photos in junk shops and flea markets—" but the other woman continued, without answering: "I somehow had the feeling this kid had been photographed by someone he really didn't like, in fact, a predator of some sort. I imagined this guy who had given him money to let him take photos, and then . . ."

she frowned and shuddered, and there was a buzz of comment and interjection around the table.

He stared at the woman, who was waving her hands around in the air. Cries and whispers all down the table. Little hysterias and cluck clucks. No one was looking his way. He stopped listening. He sipped his drink. Boring. The conversation had been wrested away, really rather impolitely—thrown on the junk heap of virtual flotsam and jetsam most conversations contributed to, day after day, year after year. Chat, chat, chat. Yada, yada. If only people actually listened to themselves.

He excused himself and went to the bathroom, where he stared into his own reflection with faint revulsion—he did not ask himself why, whether disappointment in all those idiot listeners or in the growing network of wrinkles on his neck, the swelling looseness under the chin—telling himself, again, the story of his own misunderstood importance, a story that always began with the phrase "no one understands me."

Hopscotch Girl

In the daily contest at recess, Alyce always won, while around
them the circle of girls bent in, breathing, grinning, whispering.
Nobody ever objected to Alyce's foot on the line, or the quick
slide-back, or some foot-shimmy shuffle scooting her into the
right square that Danika could see, clear as clear, she'd missed.
Seemed like some kind of lie made up of schoolyard air and
Alyce's sharp laugh and back row giggles made everyone else
except Danika see Alyce's foot carried from where it wasn't to
where it needed to go as though it had landed there, no doubt
about it. Alyce would twirl in the air at the double squares, hair
flying, and land. Wrong. One toe over the line. "Look! Unfair!"
Danika yelled at first, and pointed, but no one even looked at
her. Alyce had a way with her. Going against her meant
whispered giggles and nasty glances. But every day Danika tried
to win. She planted every landing, her feet solid in the air of
those boxes. A free feeling—that whirl, that touchdown.
Stepping through the precise boxed planets of her flight. But
Alyce always won, the clapping and smiles all hers.

The unfairness of it. So when and if, ever, she finally won—and she knew she would—she would stand, with her hands on her hips, grinning the very grin Alyce had been preparing for her own face, while everyone giggled and pointed as Alyce stomped off glowering.

Also she'd tell her mother, who had said, when Danika talked about the daily injustice, "Relax, honey. No point getting yourself in an uproar about something like this! Godssake, no one can cheat at hopscotch, it's too simple." She'd tell her mother then, simple or complicated, Alyce did cheat, and every day, but now she, Danika, was the Queen of daily hopscotch.

One day after the game Alyce came up to her when the other girls had wandered off. Danika was standing by herself staring down at the chalk grid. Alyce grinned and leaned close. "Hey" she hissed, "the real trick isn't the jumping anyway, Dennie"— no one called Danika Denny—" the thing is the lagger stones." Danika stared, kept her mouth shut. She didn't move. Alyce told her the good stones just skipped and soared home to where they belonged, and they helped what people saw, too. So throwing the stones right, that was the hard part. She laughed, a knowing chortle. She knew a secret place, she said, the best place, to find them. She folded her arms and her grin grew wider as though her jaw was being stretched by the favor she was doing Danika, as though Danika had complained again or asked for help from her, the expert, even though she hadn't said anything at all, just watched as Alyce as usual stepped on a line on her final hop, but still won, surrounded by the clapping and mean little purrs of the others. "So. There you are," said Alyce. She skipped off.

So that afternoon, as it was getting on dusk, Danika followed Alyce on her way home, quiet as quiet, into the tangly hedgerow next to Farmer Frisk's field., careful not to crackle any sticks or get too close. Alyce ran ahead and branched off into what looked like a rabbit-sized path lined with scratchies and tightly massed branches and quickly disappeared. Danika saw paths everywhere, branching every whichway. So to make sure she could find her way home, she tore up the note her mother had left that morning saying she'd be home late and threw the small bits of paper down on the path behind her. It got darker.

Suddenly, up ahead, she heard Alyce laugh. Then in a dark flash

she was running straight back toward Danika. Her face seemed

huge, like a moon; they were going to collide. But she whipped

by, brushing Danika and kicking up a sharp wind—it felt hot and

sharp like berry prickles. A blizzard of paper bits whirled away

into the trees. But Danika pushed on by herself as the night grew

darker, looking down on the path and into the trees for good

stones. She wouldn't turn around yet, though she wasn't sure

where to look. She thought she saw a light up ahead. She thought

she heard an owl. Or was it a car? A growl? She turned, but the

paper bits were all gone. Was that breathing behind her? She was

not at home when her mother returned.

The next day, Danika was missing, and Alyce won the contest as

usual.

That Moment

She looked at him. He looked at her. That looking moment did it.

Do you know what I mean? Something winged its way between

them, not just desire, but something made up of a sudden wind of

knowledge no one else besides these two could feel, a breeze

made up of a thousand invisible eyes, something not even skin

could explain, a word in a language only they two understood, a

place, a shimmer of a world holding them together in the green

or wind or smudge of reality's smoke.

This flew between them, making one of those airtight bridges

that can span (almost) all weathers. I wouldn't say all, no, but

luck will tell, I suppose, whether this bridge builds a pathway

that keeps opening again and again, no matter the brambles. It's

a thicket world, yes.

But at the moment we're holding here, there's no doubt. He

looks at her. She looks at him. (Forget the gender, it's all the same animal beauty.) And then. It unfolds, and if they're lucky,

the ripple out makes love fertile, so its forest spreads.

This we want and sometimes make.

Let Us Entertain

Let us entertain (the us that's I and you, the writer making and the reader making) the idea that thought (right here in this head where I'm thinking it, or in yours where you are) is not words but some state or medium of which words are merely one precipitate - action, another.

Both thought and feeling (which may not be distinct - cognition's an ignition can never but be flooded with the colors of joy, rue, anger, elation, sadness, and all those others for whom the words must be built up on an architecture of inexact and indirect mapping) are founded on sensation.

Without sensation (our sensate bodies) we'd have no thoughts or feelings, not the neurons or the myths either. It's with sensation that we feel ourselves and the world apart from us, and from the rippled music of this vibration sounding comes feeling/thought, however these heavenly twins are birthed.

The idea that they are separate (thought and feeling) defies imagination, literally, though not philosophy, which is so often a system of categorization (i.e. dissection). Have you tried to think without feeling? (Oh, you think you have?--what's the characteristic tone to the "I would like to reject the thought that I must feel when I think or vice-versa" thought, the grayish, obstinate feel? or the whisper of discourse or formulation that comes with the hungry feeling, or the blank feeling, or the I'm-not-thinking-anything-at-all-at-the-moment feeling?)

Does it tickle, this thought, or rub you the wrong way? See what I mean?

But back to the thought is not words idea. Maybe it's only that words are not synonymous with thought, and vice versa. Thought can be a wordless act, even a pictureless act -- the electricity inside, thought's ladders & motions-- while you read these very words, perhaps. The feeling and cognitive embrace with which

you surround and respond to these words
even as you read them is not
necessarily or even usually
wholly verbal, right in the very
mouth of language, as words
wing in. You may stop to have a
thought or a series of ideas which
are almost or immediately
translated into words, and the
passage from non-verbal thought to verbal
thought may be instantaneous
and in some synaptic way without
barrier (or the sequence may
read from verbal to non-verbal,
with transliteration occurring
colored or blooming from north to south to
east to west) but some significant
portion of thought (my thought at
least, which is all I'm privy to)--
despite my passion for word and
for the conversion of
thought/feeling states into word
is not in language but in a
precisely and elegantly weighted
(to both language and interiority)
soup of sensate/feel/idea
mapping that is multiplicitous
and takes place in an interior
geography of a design not quite
like the maps we make of planar
surfaces.

More you might say like story or dreams or
the backyard converted into
poem. And not always in a
language of the spoken or written
kind, although highly graphed or
textualized by words, but
including a placeness that is

more global and less linear than language. Language is the fire's smoke, or, sometimes, the skin that rises to its heat.

Language is a tongue with which we lick the world. the palm, the fingers reaching. it is a globe, you know. and you knew, didn't you, I meant the irresistible, the wordless and beloved, the world?

(Up the left side of this page there is, in the original, a blue column ending in a squiggly line which carries you off the page and into non-word space).

~Five~ How

The Small of the Year

So fine is sometimes always. This of course was provisional with us. That Fall we tried it, night after night, under the covers, and so far, so fine.

It was his certain gaze and way of yes that did it, actually. And he could make such a yes of me—he had a handsome method, pioneer. Outside the moon waxed and waned in a very shiny way. Simply white sheets. I noticed everything about him I could. It went the other way, too; he called himself a fine-toothed comb.

Then always was not the point. The point was always then, and again. I forgot to think, I think, though my mother had tried to prepare for this by packing in a certain thought like same sardines, over and over, in the oil of bored evenings and drilling lectures. "Don't forget your head's upstairs," she'd say. "Don't try to think with what's downstairs, it's by and large an idiot." So I didn't think with any idiots, but dreamed with handy skin.

"Here," he'd say, "try this." The habit of trying came quick, because trying often came out well, and long.

It was not summer, and in addition I was not eighteen or an any bumpkin or budnut. I was well into high noon, that median strip, and my job, and of course my father.

My father's ungrateful future had crept into his spine, 3rd and 4th lumbar vertebrae, and started a spreading gnaw. Out the ribs, jumped to pelvis. The doctors looked sharkish, though wearing a bedside manner. Legions and militia marshalled minor Punic wars inside me, mostly daytime. I was trying a lot. On the phone my father kept at it, warning me about the wrong time to eat mussels, Oxalis in the grass, forgetting flowers for my mother's grave. A long November lessened slowly but listed toward December.

I tried and tried through familiar days. Also and with regular intermittence, the fine nights cradled me. Awakening was often evening.

My father was telling me about Oxalis and a ghost. "It's impossible to root out," he said, "once it gets started." He ignored the tubes and straps and all the fierce white and waved his arms, signifying roots, perseverance, danger. "It's incredibly well adapted, strong root systems, little bulbet things that winter over and multiply like crazy. Once it flowers you've had it, so I'm telling you, buster, get it out of your lawn." Buster's not my name or even my gender, but that's my father for you.

"Don't worry about the Oxalis, Dad," I said, "for god's sake." "It's as good as anything, don't you think?" he answered. "Answer me that one. Oxalis is as good as the next worry, I myself would certainly say, I don't know about you, and anything's possible if you catch it in time." Arguing was of course, but often off course, so I didn't.

The ghost appeared in the evening he said, it was moon timing. As soon as thigs got blue he could expect a visit. "Oh you don't know what I mean really because ghost isn't the word, but that's what it is. There's nothing wrong with me. Don't move that, I want it right there. It's Barbara, of course. She doesn't have much to say, and I wish she'd speak up when she does. She mumbles. I'm deaf." He poked at the bed controls. "You need a pilot's license nowadays to be sick. What are you making for Thanksgiving? Pecan, or raisin?" Year after year, I made pecan pie, because they all liked it. I like raisin. "Dad," I said, "are you always going to hold it against me, that I can't see the superiority of the pecan over the raisin?" It must have been my tone. "I don't know," he said, and gave me that look. "Maybe you know about always, if you're so smart. Not me."

Best I could do was one thing after another, counting this and that the way they lined up. Night and day breathed in different directions, like Siamese twins, but between them only one heart. The body's not a narrow thing when you think how far, through what, it stretches, and as a continent it carries sweep. My father was in the dismissing stage. "Take this," he'd say. "I don't want it any more." His hands folded easily, dropped down out of motion with thankful wrists. "I enjoy these evening talks," he'd say, "even though she mumbles."

After all Thanksgiving was pecan, as usual. As usual may be as always as you get.

Dad and Jackson never met. Dad said now was not the time for him to start something new, the trip home for the meal was just about as far as he could stretch it, God knows he wished me luck, and Jack said yeah never mind cranberry was the least of it. Dad and Stevie and Justin and Trina ate the turkey and the pie and watched the blue begin. To me blue announced either Barbara or Jackson. These exits, they're revolving doors.

When you know something's going to happen it surprises you when it finally does. Because you're always waiting which fools you into thinking you've prepared when you've merely fidgeted around trying to get settled in a place you know is only temporary. Now, pecan pies are something I miss, not because I like them. After all the all seems larger, at least in this case. He never mumbled, and I miss it sometimes.

In the small of the year ghosts come, small after years. This, along with the usual raisin, adds to the festivities. Jack regrets now not meeting Dad because he says then he could better unpick the many strands. The long nights always remind me, and the moon. In the small of the year so fine's not always but still usual with us.

How The Moon Grew Various

At first the moon was always round, fat as a penny, like the sun, only at night and silver. She was famous and had a perpetual nature. This was ago, before things changed.

At night, when Fox hunted, he couldn't keep his eyes off her; this made it difficult to pay attention properly to food and its ambulations. Her silver was not like his, mixed and made up of many; it was an always color and knocked on his eye. Sometimes, when he was passing from tree shadow into the windows she made on the ground, the hair there on the back of his neck would rise with the sheerness. He had to go into the dark, deep under the trees, to piss and sleep and even to eat. After a while he was getting thin. Hunting her didn't fill his belly but he couldn't stop. Night after night she sailed right into his song.

Loving her with his belly and teeth and the long hairs on the back of his neck, he couldn't bear not being able to touch her, but all his running on ridges and every clever leap failed.

So Fox who was well known for clever and could make much out of little and vice versa thought something up. He went into the back of his cave and gathered together the shreds of bone under darkness behind rocks and in back, and he sewed them together to make a cloak. The cloak had a look like the unders of things, dark as dark, and it knew how to muffle, since it was made of thickness of nothing. Fox took it up to the highest that very night it was made.

The moon she grinned wide behind him and began as usual to laugh her way up. While she was still just touching the ridge he threw the cloak round her—it ate up her brightness like ink or fog—and gathered her in like a skein of fishes. She struggled and struggled, but once in the bag it's always too late. So he carried her home in his sack like a chicken, round and almost too light to bear. A piece of her shining fell through the mouth of the cloak on to his shoulder. It was ice and fire and made him tremble like jewels.

At home he put her there in the deep dark at the back of the cave. She shone right in his eyes, and all day too. Now Fox was happy. He slept in her light, and dreamed the brightest of dreams, all silver spoons, fishes and wishbones picked brilliant clean, and at night he hunted again. He went here and there and there and here in the easy dark, and he could follow his nose again, no distraction to teeth or his clever eyes, and so he grew sleek.

But she was terribly lonely, for the stars, for the looking down into greatness, for the sky's hands and shoulders. She was too round and too bright for the back of a cave. So she made a magic, one made not of darkness but all of bright. She cut a lock of her hair, long sliver of silver, and made a bargain with Bat. Now Bat was normally king of invisible, not a creature for appearance, even in tales, but Bat was disgruntled and his normal distaste for signature or contract was offset by this dreadful high noon at the back of the cave. Shyly, he'd always thought well of the moon, but now she was too close for comfort, and not liking her asleep there at all, all that terrible absence of dark in the daytime, Bat was ready even to speak in his little reed of a voice. He hovered, eyes turned hard inward, in the most shadow of rock, and they struck a bargain. So Bat, whose flying was smooth and longer than any ladder or bird, took her hair sliver up high and high and laid the lick of it way up in the top of the sky. Next night she made the next and Bat laid it longside the other just like nesting a spoon. Next and next till the sliver grew almost half.

A bit and Fox noticed the dwindle and flare, a strange coming and going almost like now, and saw she was stealing herself back. He who was known for parley and wheedle begged and then anger, but she only stole from herself as before. "You are the thief," she said. "My wholeness is mine, and belongs to the sky." Then she clipped and chipped more till up sky her pieces made almost a roundness and down cave her brightness lay thin, glimmering only.

Near the most roundness above she lay in the cave, almost eaten
to nothing. Even Bat, whose dusk in the cave had come back,
was afraid. She couldn't give Bat the last, because she would die
and dark in the cave then and dark in the sky. Fox saw this, but
also he saw how his lady and love was not there and not here.
He had her but didn't.

She knew it too, lying there changed in spite of her freedoms.
So because things were not as they once, they had to agree on a
newness. The bargain they made took up going and coming, so
that even the sea learned yearning and wander.

They agreed she would live one night every month in his cave,
bright as her shine original, and one night in such roundness
afloat in the sky, and all other nights she would dance slowly
open and turn slowly closed. As for Bat, he lived in the cave
with the coming and going and studied the difference between
appearance and apparition. He took to hanging upside down,

nested kin to kin in a series like spoons, as though copying with

his little black body a sliver of light.

So it went as it does now, the moon become various, Fox living

in night light and darkness all mixed. It's a long, old story.

Sometimes he knew her or found her; sometimes she sailed

herself, and that was now, too.

Tobey Hiller writes in multiple genres. Her flash, stories and poems appear in numerous publications and anthologies. She's the author of four books of poems, a novel, and a collection of surreal stories; her most recent books are *Flight Advice: A Fabulary* and *Crow Mind*. She has recently completed a new collection of realist stories, and her current poetry manuscript, *before anything is dust*, was a finalist in Catamaran Literary Readers annual Poetry Book Contest. Her poetry has been nominated for a Pushcart Prize. She lives in Northern California with her husband, happy to be on the western edge near creeks, mountains, and many interstitial creatures.

www.ingramcontent.com/pod-product-compliance
Lightning Source LLC
Chambersburg PA
CBHW060400050426
42449CB00009B/1828